POEMS OF THE ZODIAC

by

Joanna Nealon

"Sirius Fun"

Acknowledgements

The author wishes to express her deep gratitude to
Jiri Jirasek,
longtime editor of
Cosmic Trend, Ontario, CN,
which published the 1st edition of
. "Poems Of The Zodiac"
in 1992.
Further warm thanks go to
Joyce Charrey
(and Kaline Charrey, re: LEO)
for the illustrations.

IN Publications 2009
14 Lorraine Circle, Waban, MA 02468

POEMS OF THE ZODIAC

ISBN: 978-0-9819797-0-0

Introduction to the First Edition

Dear Reader,

I have written two poems for each of the twelve Sun Signs, one, a serious archetype, and the other, a more humorous stereotype, though these definitions overlap at times, according to the nature of the Sign. I confess immediately that I am a Libra, and have included three poems for my own Sign. This aberration did not spring from pride. True to the incorrigible indecisiveness of Libra, I was constitutionally unable to choose two out of the three poems which sparked my imagination!

A word on the use of personal pronouns: You Lady Rams, for instance, may resent being referred to as "he", and, likewise, you Gentlemen Bulls may "see red" being referred to as "she". Yet such is the way of Astrology, as it is the Ruler of the Sign which dictates the gender of the pronoun. Fire and Air are designated "Masculine Day Signs", but may have a feminine ruler, such as Venus, who presides over Libra. Earth and Water are designated "Feminine Night Signs", but may have a masculine Ruler, such as Mercury, who presides over Virgo.

There are profound esoteric reasons behind the nomenclature of Astrology, too far reaching to explore in the preface to a volume which is, for the most part, "Sirius" fun!

Joanna Nealon

THE TWELVE CONSTELLATIONS OF THE ZODIAC AND THEIR RULERS

1
Aries, The Ram
Fire Sign, ruled by Mars

2
Taurus, The Bull
Earth Sign, ruled by Venus

3
Gemini, The Twins
Air Sign, ruled by Mercury

4
Cancer, The Crab
Water Sign, ruled by The Moon

5
Leo, The Lion
Fire Sign, ruled by The Sun

6
Virgo, The Virgin
Earth Sign, ruled by Mercury

THE TWELVE CONSTELLATIONS OF THE ZODIAC
AND THEIR RULERS

7
Libra, The Scales
Air Sign, ruled by Venus

8
Scorpio, The Scorpion or The Eagle (when transformed)
Water Sign, ruled by Mars and Pluto

9
Sagittarius, The Archer
Fire Sign, ruled by Jupiter

10
Capricorn, The Goat
Earth Sign, ruled by Saturn

11
Aquarius, The Water Bearer
Air Sign, ruled by Uranus

12
Pisces, The Fish
Water Sign, ruled by Neptune

ARIES
JC 6.30.91

ARIES

Aries, the Ram, with flaming horns,
His questing head held high,
Strikes his stance on the hill of hope
Against the April sky.

His proud Ram's head is battle-scarred,
For he is a fighter bold,
Butting his horns against the world
And refusing to grow old!

His love is fierce, but fiercer still
Is his explosive ire.
The Ram's wrath chills, but his love ensouls
The cosmic cold with Fire.

His will is strong. His heart is true.
The Ram does not take flight.
And when his head, wisdom heeds,
His deeds are full of light.

ARIES

A slam from the Ram will knock you flat!
Suddenly he charges in the middle of a chat.

A butt from this beast, if just spoken,
Will leave your bones intact, but your heart is broken.

As your adrenaline increases,
The Ram's wrath ceases, and he helps pick up your pieces.

For the Ram's not the sort to hold a grudge.
Yes, you made him mad, and you received a nasty nudge.

But when you've been whammed, properly goddamned,
The Ram becomes a Lamb, and your wish is his command.

Yes, restive Ram or Lamb in the manger,
Gregarious Aries is well worth the danger!

TAURUS

JC 7.14.91

TAURUS

Night-eyed, tender Taurus
Has the grave glance of Venus on the Earth,
Where far from realms of Air,
She links love's pulse to pain and human birth.

Earth-stubborn, but content,
She confounds and vexes volatile Fire.
Yet her serene repose
Does not repress Earth's rich deeps of desire.

The mind's airy cartwheels
Cannot stir the pools of her placid eyes,
Where Love waits and suffers,
Lone Evenstar, before the heart's sunrise.

TAURUS

Taurus will not budge an inch.
Push her, pull her, even pinch!

Beautiful, dependable,
But she is unbendable.

Taurus in her stubborn mode
Hates the goad and may implode.

She is soft-eyed, full of sleep,
Princess of Earth's dreaming deep.

But she wakes up with a start
If jealous darts disturb her heart.

Taurus is a tiger then.
Does not even count to ten.

No more slow benign bovine,
But Venus in a wrath divine!

Yet if Taurus is not riled,
She is tender, true, and mild,

Her strong firm feet, standing ground,
Her gaze, peaceful and profound.

GEMINI

GEMINI

Cool-eyed Mercury, gleaming wizard,
Who wields the dual wands of Gemini,
Makes manifest Man's divine blueprint,
His classic symmetry, sketched on high.

Keen master of cosmic counterpoise,
With quicksilver glance of clarity,
He sees past the pain of paradox
To the place beyond polarity.

Human eyes, wise gift of Gemini, *
Uniquely focused for Man's seeing,
Are Spirit's windows on the world of sense,
Where shines the gaze of conscious being.

* There might be some who contend that the eyes are formed under
the constellation of Aries, which rules the human head, but,
ultimately, all symmetry belongs to the realm of The Twins. Gemini
rules thinking and communication, which is related to Man's
symmetric form, upright stance, and visual focus, necessary
conditions for the incarnation of the human ego.

GEMINI

Man's temple of celestial symmetry
Was built by two ingenious gods,
Twin architects of complex Gemini,
Identical, and yet at odds.

So he, the Mercury-born, must balance
Polarities of left and right,
Caught between cosmic contradictions
As different as are day and night.

Agile Mercury juggles joy and woe,
Wisdom and folly, fast and slow,
And all in the wink of four Gemini eyes,
A simultaneous "yes" and "no"!

It seems to you he's one of the two,
But he also is the other.
And just when you think you have met the one,
You are talking to his brother.

But duality is delightful.
It has the spice of variety.
Only one set of traits is tiresome,
Even the trait of piety.

And wizardly Mercury has the wit
To master the totality,
To solve the old riddle of light and dark,
Which is the soul's reality.

CANCER

6.29.91

CANCER

Madcap and mournful Moon dancer,
She, Cancer, sees in the lunar light,
The soul's riddle, but no answer,
The heart's naked need in the world night.

She spent her tender Moonchild years
Inside a fragile fairy palace,
Drinking in tears, Moondreams, and fears,
That spilled from a silver chalice.

Now the shy Moon maid deceives you
In her crab shell of grown-up protection,
While all the time she perceives you
With Cancer's uncanny detection.

The Moon-soft luminosity
Of her liquid eyes, fitted for Night,
Is filled with curiosity
For the mystery of Midsummer light.

Born on the eve of cosmic Day,
She, chaste Queen of the wisdom of old,
Silver and pearl as her array,
Heralds the glory of summer gold.

CANCER

Mothers, flags, and apple-pies,
Tears that dim their tender eyes.

Bank accounts and bellies full,
Winter underwear of wool.

Torsos tending towards the flabby,
Moods, Moon-crazy, cautious, crabby!

Hard hats worn to all affairs,
Under them soft cuddly bears.

Warriors for daily bread,
Babies when they're sick in bed.

Crab shells that are hard as rocks,
Sensitives in shoes and socks.

Cancerians play many parts,
Moon clowns hiding trembling hearts.

LEO KC 1991

LEO

Leo's heart is the summer Sun,
New ether-sphere of Love begun.

No brazen outer dazzle this,
Nor rays of basking, selfish bliss,

But light as gentle as Love's touch,
And never shining overmuch.

If Leo's blaze becomes too bright,
Triumphant shine of his own might,

Then is the place of summer's heart
Empty and dark, and has no part

In the macrocosmic heart of Man,
That wills to beat beyond world's span,

Bearer of quintessential worth,
The heart of resurrected Earth.

LEO

Sun-maned, magnificent Cat of all cats,
King, removed from petty feline spats,

Is Leo, Lion-heart, whose splendid chest
Ripples with the rhythmic swell of breast,

Where blood and breath, ruled by the Sun's great round,
Through his sleek and perfect body pound.

The sun-gold gaze of his complacent eye,
Mirror of calm majesty on high,

Is confident and smugly self-contained,
Knowing that its rule will be maintained

Through Leo's power as a living part
Of the pulsing, macrocosmic heart.

Yet he, by lordly generosity,
Softens Leonine pomposity!

In the kingly breast which has conquered pride,
Magnanimity and grace reside.

VIRGO

Restless and quicksilver ruled, but schooled by duty,
Is Virgo, celestial servant sent to Earth,
Preserver of holy order and high beauty,
His swift mercurial eye discerning worth.

Last bearer of the precious gifts of the past,
Yet preparer of the way that is unknown,
A voice crying in the wilderness, outcast,
Is Virgo, living in desertlands alone.

He wears Man's future countenance, the Virgin's face,
Grave and beautiful visage, yet to be won,
Human feeling illumined by wisdom's grace,
The soul of the new Sophia, lit by Sun.

VIRGO

"Cogito ergo sum," a Virgo likes to hum.
"I think, therefore, I am," though thinking makes him glum.

For the mind's inspection reveals imperfection,
And all misdirection by Virgo needs correction!

He, on Mercury's wings, is swift to size up things,
But Virgo's vitriol stings as he ties up life's loose strings.

His logic never swerves. His nitpicking unnerves.
And yet he humbly serves by the order he preserves.

Mercury is mental, his soul, transcendental,
His eyes, cool and gentle, his passion, incidental.

Life is an equation, feeling an invasion,
Though he, on occasion, succumbs to love's persuasion.

For Virgo is not cold, just too self-controlled.
And his kind deeds, never told, make Mercury pure gold!

LIBRA
AC 7.12.91

LIBRA

Beautiful lady, Libran-born,
Autumn's Queen, holds the winter in scorn.

Wrapped in her robe of sunset glow,
Coral and rose, to oppose the snow,

She lights the hearth for winter's span,
Fanning the flame in the soul of Man.

Libra, goddess of lambent Air,
Bright Michaelmas daisies in her hair,

Is a festive soul, and yet sober,
The mood of mellow gold October.

LIBRA

Libra is swinging on her Scales,
And she see-saws up and down.
The wind blows soft, and then in gales,
And billows her hair and gown.

Oh, she is a rocking riddle!
Will she answer yes or no?
Or will she stay in the middle,
Not knowing which way to go?

But there in the windless center,
If Libra is standing still,
Indecision will torment her
And weaken her autumn will.

Poised on the middle pole,
She scans the October sky,
Descrying a sign for her soul
Where sparks of meteors fly.

If she can behold the vision
Of St. Michael, Libra's lord,
Then she will make a decision
And forge her will like a sword!

LIBRA

Libra likes to tease, and Libra likes to please.
Libra says, "God bless you" every time you sneeze.

Libra is a liberal, a democratic soul,
Always for the lowest on life's totem-pole.

Libra lives in air, is hardly even there,
Just a beamy smile or a dreamy stare.

And Libra loves to talk, much more than work or walk.
Only rank injustice will make Libra balk.

Fairness is for Libra a "raison-d'être",
To ponder pros and cons, while mumbling "peut-être".

Libra is a poet with a sense of duty,
Servant of bright Venus, queen of love and beauty.

SCORPIO

bC 3.23.92

SCORPIO

Scorpio's cool water-silk eyes,
Masked orbs of subtly shifting light,
Conceal the sorcerer's deep surmise,
Pluto's mastery over night.

No flicker of surprise or pain
Will cross his careful, friendly face,
Though other hearts could not contain
The soul deeps in that hidden place.

The Scorpion, with sullen pride,
Loves secrets for secret's sake,
But the Eagle, ranging far and wide,
Wings back with wisdom in his wake.

Knowledge is the Eagle's power,
But never his own possession,
And at the propitious hour,
He proclaims it, with discretion.

Stronger than wisdom is his will,
That can tame his fierce emotion
And consecrate his artful skill
To high service, with devotion.

SCORPIO

Scorpio won't let you know
That he knows that you may know!
Puller of strings behind life's show,
Scorpio won't let them go.

Eagle-eyed, with noble pride,
He will listen, not confide.
No wiser or more gracious guide,
If Pluto's will be not denied.

He can master any role,
Tease you, scare you, or cajole,
And quell with velvet self-control
Scorpio's volcanic soul.

With eyes fashioned in far skies,
He sees through illusion's lies,
An Eagle in a serpent's guise,
Bird of Heaven, worldly wise.

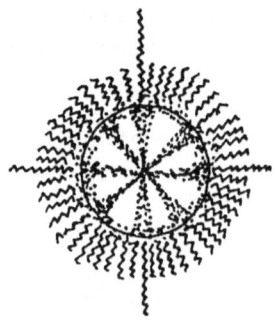

SAGITARIUS
XC 5.92

SAGITTARIUS

Jupiter's joyous countenance is kind,
Reflection of his sun-illumined mind.

He bends his bow, and with his skyward eyes
Sees where his fleet and earnest arrow flies.

His famed archery is not a child's game.
No less than truth is his ambitious aim.

And though he miss the mark, he does not cease
To try to split life's apple of caprice,

And find inside its paradox and pain
The reasons why bright Hope should not be slain!

SAGITTARIUS

Sagittarius, philosopher and clown,
Bright-eyed Jupiter, has joy for a crown.

With power in his thigh and his Archer's aim,
He pulls back his bow and plays the cosmic game!

His swift shaft pierces Heaven's startled eye,
So that holy tears run down the stricken sky.

The keen edge of his curiosity
Wounds patient wisdom with its velocity.

But kind Jupiter, of expansive heart,
Weeps huge, candid tears for his too hasty dart.

And after grief has cleansed his skyward sight,
Lifts his bow again to truth's elusive light.

CAPRICORN

CAPRICORN

Grave Saturn's stern and steady tread
Fills lighter souls than his with dread.

So fiery and airy mirth
Sobers before serious Earth.

But shy Saturn, though not witty,
Has Earth-wise eyes, full of pity.

Capricorn knows our human need
And does the selfless Father-deed,

Giving his being, granite sound,
As world foundation, will's firm ground.

While we, unwitting here above,
Walk on the patient stone of love.

CAPRICORN

Born Capricorn, he's full of scorn
For dreamers and idealists.
The Goat prefers cash-registers
And self-reliant realists.

A car that purrs, his wife in furs,
The children all in college;
No dramatics, no fanatics,
No cults, no occult knowledge!

His crew-cut hair makes people stare.
There's no doubting Saturn's sex.
His suits are dully suitable,
With no shouting stripes or checks.

Views archaic, muse prosaic,
Yet with common sense profound,
He slowly climbs up hills of dimes,
With his conscience as sure ground.

Cut from Saturn's classic pattern,
He's as old as Father Time,
Patient, steady, patriarchal,
And unconsciously sublime.

AQUARIUS

AQUARIUS

Aquarius, wearer of the human face,
And Water Bearer to the human race,

Is borne by the Wind, his intimate friend,
To fetch water from the well at world's end,

Water to purify thinking's stagnation,
Sprinkling parched souls with Imagination!

Bright Air intermingles water and sun,
Etheric heart of a new world begun.

AQUARIUS

The winds of Aquarius are always various,
Furious, curious, sad, and hilarious!

The far skies of his eyes are full of surprises,
Swift lightnings, laughter, and a dozen disguises.

There are days when a dull glaze will cloud his clear glance,
As the mind behind it does a weird cosmic dance.

The airborne Aquarian neither sees nor hears.
In the head's giddy heights, the whole world disappears.

But the lofty Uranus does not disdain us
And swoops back to Earth with fresh thoughts to sustain us.

He has heard Heaven's plans, the latest creations,
Then astounds and confounds with his innovations!

He brings bright tomorrows into long gray todays,
As he ventures alone through the spirit's vast maze.

PISCES

JC 92

PISCES

Pisces, silent swimmer,
Swift blur of elusive motion,
A soft, silver shimmer
In soul's abysmal ocean,

Is Neptune's neophyte,
Diver into the mystic deep,
Where in ancient twilight
The solemn mysteries sleep.

Sea-eyed Pisces perceives
What no outer sun illumines,
While Water's murk deceives
The dry Earth-eyes of humans.

Fish, last constellation,
On the way of the souls of men,
Returns for revelation
To the sacred sea again.

PISCES

Just try to find out who he is,
The secretive and slippery Fish!
Now you see 'im, now you don't.
Sly Pisces exits with a swish.

Neptune taught him all his tricks,
This underwater acrobat.
In subterranean retreats,
The Fish eludes familiar chat.

Pisces likes his privacy,
Yet he can be convivial.
And he attends when YOU tell all
To matters great and trivial.

The Fish is fond of listening
To sagas, sad and witty.
Tales of woe will overflow
His liquid eyes with love and pity.

He is a weary traveler.
Twelve journeys lie behind his eyes.
Pisces is a sea-old soul,
Impervious to all surprise.

ABOUT THE POET

Once upon a time on October 16, under the constellation of Libra, I entered the world. Needless to say, the years I have spent on this planet have been fraught with indecision, but never indifference. The one unshakable decision I have made is to keep on striving to understand the "why" of human existence, so inextricably bound up with the Cosmos. Popular astrology is a remnant of an ancient high wisdom, the divining of super-sensible realities which underlie the physical Universe.

Long ago I received a B.A. in French literature and studied in Paris, France on a Fulbright Scholarship. After that I was eclipsed by the natural and happy outcome of marriage, three children. The child-raising years were absorbing and demanding, as for all attentive parents, but perhaps more so for my husband and me, as we are both blind.

For years I stacked my poems in my heart, until my husband, Kenneth Ingham, Ph.D., a computer scientist, placed a talking-terminal at my disposal, and my fingers flew over the keys. Finally, in 1987, I began circulating poetry and reciting in the Boston area, mainly with the Stone Soup Poetry Group, founded by poet, Jack Powers, in 1971. My first book, "The Lie And I", was published in 1990 by Stone Soup Press.

Then, in 1992, I had the great good fortune to have "Poems of the Zodiac" published by Cosmic Trend, Ontario, CN. Since then I have had three more books published, SAID THE SAGE, 1993, by New Spirit Press; THE FOURTH KINGDOM, 1998, by Cosmic Trend; and LIVING IT, 2004, by Ibbetson Street Press. I have continued to recite poetry in affiliation with various on-going venues in Massachusetts, such as Tapestry Of Voices, Ibbetson Street Review, Brockton Library Series, Walden Pond Series, and Chapter and Verse. Also, since 1992 I have participated in poetry programs at Bay State and Norfolk Prisons.

As they say in astrological parlance,
"Scratch a Libra and get a poet!"

Joanna Nealon

www.ingramcontent.com/pod-product-compliance
Lightning Source LLC
Chambersburg PA
CBHW021914040426
42447CB00007B/861